We gratefully acknowledge permission to reprint the following poems:

Poem of the Week

**50 Irresistible Poems With Activities
That Teach Key Reading & Writing Skills
. . . and Inspire a Love of Poetry All Year Long!**

Selected by Maria Fleming

S C H O L A S T I C
PROFESSIONAL BOOKS

New York • Toronto • London • Auckland • Sydney
Mexico City • New Delhi • Hong Kong

Cover design by Jaime Lucero
Cover illustration by Laura Merer
Interior design by Sydney Wright
Interior illustration by James Graham Hale

ISBN: 0-439-07751-6

Table of Contents

Table of Contents (cont.)

Introduction

Poets are a lot like architects. A poet carefully chooses and positions each word to give shape and meaning to a poem, like a builder artfully laying bricks to form a snug house. Who better than these word masons to unlock for children the mysteries and the power and the beauty of language?

It's no secret that children love and respond to poetry, delighting in its rhythm and rhyme. *Poem of the Week* will help you tap into that natural interest to promote students' language development and stimulate their curiosity about the world around them. In this book, you'll find poems that will take you through each week of the school year, from September to June. There are poems about the seasons and special days; poems about favorite animals such as bugs, bears, and penguins; and poems that center around tried-and-true primary-grade themes such as friendship, weather, colors, and plants.

Making a Place for Poetry

There are many ways to use the poetry selections in this book. Dip into the book throughout the year, whenever you're looking for a special poem to launch a theme unit, commemorate a holiday, or develop a language arts lesson on a particular skill. Poetry moves easily across the curriculum. Use the poems to launch lessons in art, music, drama, science, math, and social studies. Preceding each selection are activities to help you get the most curricular mileage out of a poem. You may want to make a special ritual out of sharing the poems by setting aside a particular day and time each week to introduce a new selection. Create a Poetry Corner with an easel and chart pad. Every Monday, you can write a new poem on a piece of chart paper and keep it on display for the week. Return to the poem again and again during the course of the week to introduce and reinforce different language arts skills. Because the poems are rich in alliteration and rhyme, they offer an excellent way to build children's phonemic awareness. And the poems' repetitive and predictable language—as well as their brevity—can help boost students' confidence as readers. Children may want to decorate the poetry corner with artwork they create in response to each week's selection. They may also want to add to the display poems they find in other books or write themselves.

You can also stock learning centers with copies of the poems or use them as the centerpiece for bulletin-board displays. Students might enjoy making audio recordings of the poems for a listening center. Send copies home for students to read and discuss with family members for additional language arts enrichment. You're sure to find countless other ways to enrich your curriculum with the poetry selections in this book.

Poetry Reading Tips

When you introduce a poem, read it through once in its entirety, without pausing, so that students can hear the rhythm and music of the language. Allow time for

children to share their spontaneous reactions: How does the poem make them feel? What did they like or dislike about it? Were there any groups of words that tickled their ear? What pictures did the poem make them see in their heads?

Then, when appropriate, spend a few minutes focusing on some of the techniques the poet uses. The "Poetry Pointers" and "Inspirations" that proceed each selection offer further tips for reading and examining poetic techniques such as alliteration, simile, metaphor, personification, onomatopoeia, and more. Depending on students' age and ability level, you may or may not decide to use the technical terms for these devices. But even if young children don't comprehend the terminology, they will intuitively grasp the concepts. After all, the poet's tools—observing the world closely with the five senses, making comparisons, experimenting with the sound and meaning of words—are the same ones young children use to understand and interpret their own universe. And sharing poetry frequently with students, and offering them a glimpse into the poet's craft, will enable even young children to transfer what they learn about language to their own writing.

Poetry has tremendous potential to teach, tickle, and inspire young learners. We hope the selections, activities, and reading tips in this book will provide the resources you need to weave poetry through your curriculum, every week of the school year.

September

First Day of School

Poetry Pointers

Ask students if the speaker really has butterflies flying around in his or her stomach. What does the expression "butterflies in your stomach" mean? Invite volunteers to share examples of times they have experienced that nervous, fluttery feeling. What makes them nervous about the beginning of a new school year? Ask students to compare their fears with those of the speaker in the poem. What happens in the poem that makes those fears disappear?

Inspirations

Butterfly Buddies: Here's a simple way to ease first-day-of-school jitters by helping children get to know one another. Use the reproducible on page 112 as a template for creating butterfly patterns from colored construction paper and patterned paper (wrapping paper, origami paper, wallpaper). You'll want only two butterflies in each color/pattern. Distribute the shapes randomly to children, including yourself in the activity if there is an odd number of students. Each child should then try to find the classmate who has the same butterfly color/pattern he or she does. Once students have paired up, they can interview each other to determine three things they have in common; for example, family size, favorite activity, food likes and dislikes, and so on.

So Long, Summer!: Point out to students that butterflies are a symbol of summer, and the sight of them dancing around the dogwood tree is something that the speaker will miss. Divide a piece of chart paper into two columns. Head one column "So Long, Summer!" and the other "Hello, School!" Ask children to name things they will miss about summer as well as things they are looking forward to this school year. Write each item under the appropriate column heading.

First Day of School

In summertime the butterflies
dance 'round our dogwood tree.
Now summer's done and school's begun,
they're fluttering in me!

Will my teacher like me?
Will I make new friends?
Will I learn to write my name
before the school year ends?

Look! There's my teacher now—
she winks as I walk in.
And a boy with a friendly, freckled face
just flashed me a wide grin.

We learn to write the alphabet—
and it's only the first day!
Hey, I think those butterflies
are fluttering away!

I'll see you soon, my sunny friends,
back where you belong—
dancing 'round the dogwood tree
when summer sings its song.

—Maria Fleming

At the Top of My Voice

Poetry Pointers

The brag or boast is a familiar poetic form that celebrates the speaker's unique gifts. In this poem, the writer uses exaggeration to convey the message that she is someone special. Ask students if they know what the word *exaggerate* means. Once you've established a satisfactory definition, ask students to identify the three specific boasts the poet makes and how they are examples of exaggeration. Use the poem as a springboard for a discussion on how each person is unique.

Inspirations

Getting to Know Me: Here's a good get-acquainted activity for the beginning of the school year. Ask children to draw their self-portraits on the front of brown paper lunch bags. Students may want to use yarn and other materials to accent features such as hair and eyebrows. At home, children should find and put in their bags three to four small objects that say something about who they are. For example, they might include a photograph of their family or pet, a favorite toy, a baseball card from their collection, and so on. Set aside time each day for a few students to introduce themselves to their new classmates by sharing the contents of their bags.

Me, Wonderful Me!: Children will enjoy imagining their own limitless abilities in a poetry-writing activity modeled after this selection. Begin by having children practice the art of exaggeration. Ask them to identify activities they are good at and to create a couple of sentences or sentence fragments in which they exaggerate that ability, for example:

* ✸ When I run, the wind races to catch up with me.
* ✸ When I run, the racehorses all get jealous.
* ✸ When I run, my sneakers lift off the ground and fly.

Then they can use their sentences to write poems celebrating their skills and talents. Children may feel less limited in their writing if you remind them that poems need not rhyme.

At the Top of My Voice

When I stamp
The ground thunders,
When I shout
The world rings,
When I sing
The air wonders
How I do such things.

—Felice Holman

New Friend

Poetry Pointers

This poem celebrates one of the joys of a new school year: making new friends. Ask children if they notice anything unusual about the poem and the pattern of its words and rhymes. Students may notice that each line begins with the article *A* and ends with *friend*. Also, the rhyming words are not the last word in each line but the second-to-last word. Occasionally, there is an *internal rhyme*, that is, a rhyme within a given line (i.e., *new/true* in the first line). Invite students to find the instances where these rhymes occur in the poem (lines 1, 3, 6, and 11).

Inspirations

How to Be a Friend: Use the poem to launch a discussion about what children value in a friend and the rewards of friendship. What qualities do they look for in a friend? (For example, someone who is kind, fair, knows how to share, listens, and so on.) Ask students to provide specific examples of how they can be a good friend. List all of their ideas on chart paper. Distribute magazines and ask children to look for pictures that depict the acts of friendship they have named. Use the pictures to create a class friendship collage.

Friendly Fun: What activities do children like to do with their friends? Invite students to draw pictures of themselves enjoying these activities with friends, then write or dictate sentences about their pictures. Bind their drawings and captions together to make a class book about friendship. Showcase the book in a special themed reading corner that features other books about friendship, including classics such as the *Frog and Toad* books by Arnold Lobel (HarperCollins), the *George and Martha* books by James Marshall (Houghton Mifflin), and *Ira Sleeps Over* and *Ira Says Goodbye* by Bernard Waber (Houghton Mifflin).

New Friend

A new friend, a true friend
A cheers-me-when-I'm-blue friend
A sunny-day-hurray friend
A come-over-and-play friend
A nice-in-every-way friend
A new friend, a true friend
A turns-the-gray-skies-blue friend
A talk-and-talk-non-stop friend
A giggle-till-we-drop friend
A none-can-ever-top friend
A new friend, a true friend
A happy-I-met-you friend

— Maria Fleming

Gray Squirrel

Poetry Pointers

After reading the poem, ask students if there were particular lines or groups of words that they liked the sound of. Explain to students that poets love to play with language, and they often repeat a sound to make a line or group of lines sound musical. Read the poem aloud again, and ask students what sounds they hear repeated. If children get stuck, you may want to point directly to a sound or a letter combination and ask if they see it elsewhere in the poem (for example, the *urry* sound in *hurry, scurry, furry* in lines 1 and 2; the *sc* sound in *scamper, scurry* in line 1; the *cr* sound in *crack* and *crunch* in line 3).

Inspirations

Squirrels in Action: Gray squirrels and red squirrels are common throughout the country. In the fall, take your class to an area where they can watch the lively habits of these animals. Be sure to remind students of important wildlife safety tips, such as not to feed or approach the squirrels or any other animal, but to watch silently from a short distance away. Encourage students to record observations in their science journals. What different types of behavior do they notice? (For example, playing, fighting, nest building, eating food, burying food, and so on.) Back in class, young scientists can compare their observations.

A couple of other things to keep an eye out for:

* *Squirrel Nests*...Piles of leaves high in a tree's branches. While squirrels usually sleep in dens deep inside tree trunks during the winter, they sometimes build leafy summer nests that become visible in autumn when a tree's branches are bare.

* *Squirrel Feeding*...Signs of squirrel feeding include piles of pinecone scales or nutshells.

A Nose for Nuts: In the fall, when nuts are plentiful, squirrels bury them in the ground and dig them up later when food is scarce. How do squirrels find the nuts they had buried? They sniff them out; squirrels have an excellent sense of smell. They can even find nuts buried under a layer of snow! Invite children to see if their sense of smell is as sharp as a squirrel's. Divide students into small groups. Provide each group with four paper cups that contain "mystery foods" such a chocolate candy, a strawberry, a piece of bubble gum, an orange segment, and so on. Blindfolded group members can take turns guessing what each sample is. Create a graph showing how many children guessed one, two, three, or all four samples correctly.

Gray Squirrel

Hurry, hurry, scamper, scurry,
Little squirrel all gray and furry.
Find an acorn; crack it, crunch it,
Nibble, nibble, munch, munch, munch it.
Find another, fat and round,
To bury quickly in the ground.
Gather nuts—don't stop to play!
For winter winds are on the way.

— Joan Horton

October

Autumn Leaves

Poetry Pointers

Direct students' attention to the shape of the poem. What does it remind them of? Point out that the poet placed the words on the page so that they look a bit like leaves falling to the ground. What words do students hear repeated? Here, the frequent repetition of the word *leaves*, as well as the less frequent repetition of the word *falling*, creates a kind of chant.

Inspirations

A Closer Look at Leaves: Ask children to point out the words the poet uses to describe leaves: color words, shape words, names of trees that the leaves come from. Then take your class on a leaf hunt. Ask students to collect a variety of autumn leaves that have fallen. Back in the classroom, groups of three or four kids can classify leaves according to different attributes, such as edge (pointy, smooth, etc.), color, shape, or size. Be sure to have age-appropriate field guides on hand so students can also identify the type of trees leaves have fallen from. Groups can chart their results by gluing the leaves to oak tag under appropriate category headings. For example, a chart categorizing leaves by shape might be divided into columns showing leaves shaped like mittens, stars, hearts, fans, feathers, and so on.

Autumn Mural: Fill several small bowls or shallow pans with red, orange, yellow, and brown tempera paint. Children can then dip leaves (vein side down) into the paint and press them onto a large sheet of craft paper to create leaf prints. Use the leaf-print mural as a backdrop for displaying students' own autumn-themed poetry.

Autumn Leaves

Green leaves,
  Yellow leaves,
    Red leaves, and brown,
      Falling,
        Falling,
          Blanketing the town.
            Oak leaves,
              Maple leaves,
                Apple leaves, and pear,
                  Falling,
                    Whispering,
                      "Autumn's in the air!"
                        Big leaves,
                          Little leaves,
                            Pointed leaves, and round,
                              Falling,
                                Nestling,
                                  Carpeting the ground.

—Leland B. Jacobs

On Christopher Columbus' Ship

Poetry Pointers

This poem by Sandra Liatsos highlights one of the many marvelous things about poetry: It allows you to become anyone, go anywhere, and do anything you want. The narrator of this poem imagines herself accompanying Christopher Columbus on his journey to America. Ask children if they think they would have liked to be on that ship. Why or why not?

Inspirations

Along for the Ride: What would it have been like to travel with Christopher Columbus? Tell children we have a pretty good idea because Columbus kept a ship's log in which he recorded details about his journey. Children may want to invent a name for the mouse in the poem, then create a ship's log with entries written from this tiny mascot's point of view. Before children begin this writing activity, share books with them about Columbus' journey so that their log entries are based on fact as well as imagination.

More to Explore: Discuss the daring destinations of other explorers: the moon, outer space, the Arctic and Antarctic, oceans, the rain forest, mountaintops. If children could go anywhere, where would it be? Invite students to draw pictures of themselves embarking on their adventures of choice. During sharing time, kids can show classmates their pictures and explain why they would like to visit the places they've depicted.

On Christopher Columbus' Ship

If I had been a tiny mouse
on Christopher Columbus' ship,
I would have sailed across the sea
on a very dangerous trip.
I would have heard the thunder boom
and seen the scary lightning flash.
I would have felt each giant wave
give tiny me a giant splash.
If I had been his small, wet pet
in Christopher Columbus' hand,
I would have reached America,
the beautiful and dry new land.

—Sandra Liatsos

Pumpkin Picking

Poetry Pointers

This poem includes several examples of *similes*, a comparison between two seemingly unrelated things. Ask children what the poet compares pumpkins to (*an ocean tide, a fat balloon, an orange moon*). If children need help finding the comparisons, suggest that they look for the word *like*, which is a clue that a comparison is being made. Invite students to come up with other pumpkin comparisons.

Inspirations

Sizing Up Pumpkins: Use the pumpkin templates on the reproducible on page 113 to trace pumpkins of various sizes onto orange felt. Cut out the pumpkins and arrange them in rows on a felt board to create a pumpkin patch, mixing up the different sizes. Ask children to take turns putting the pumpkins in each row in size order, first from biggest to smallest, and then from smallest to biggest. Use the lesson as an opportunity to reinforce comparative language, i.e., big, bigger, biggest, and smaller, smaller, smallest.

Pumpkin Problems: Bring in a pumpkin—or a few pumpkins of different sizes—and use it to introduce a medley of math activities. Divide students into small groups, provide each group with a pumpkin, and have them tackle one or more of the following tasks:

1. Guess the circumference, or distance around the widest part, of the pumpkin. Use a piece of string to measure the circumference, then measure the string with a ruler. Then graph and compare circumference measurements.

2. Guess the weight of the pumpkin, then weigh it. Graph and compare pumpkin weights.

3. Guess how many pumpkinseeds are inside the pumpkin. Cut off the top of the pumpkin (with adult assistance), scoop out and clean the seeds, and start counting. Then graph and compare seed totals.

Pumpkin Picking

Let's go picking in the pumpkin patch.
Now we're jiggling the old gate latch.
Gate swings wide and we step inside.
Pumpkins spread like an ocean tide.
You take the one like a fat balloon.
I'll take the one like an orange moon.
Hike to the house in fifty paces.
Then we'll carve out the pumpkin faces.

—Sandra Liatsos

Teeny Tiny Ghost

Poetry Pointers

Young children will instantly relate to this diminutive ghost's dilemma. Before reading the poem, ask them if they have ever been treated like they were too small to tackle a big job. How did it make them feel? After reading the poem, draw students' attention to its unusual rhyme scheme. Underline groups of rhyming words with different colored markers to help children identify the pattern. Compare the pattern of rhyme with that found in other poems you have read to help children see that poets use rhyme in different ways.

Inspirations

Finger-Puppet Play: Small groups of children may enjoy dramatizing the poem with finger puppets. Children can make a stand-up haunted-house puppet theater from a cereal box. They'll need adult assistance to cut off the top of the box, cut away the back of the box, and cut out a few large windows and a door. Using the cardboard that was cut away from the back of the box, students can make a roof and attach it to the top of the house shape using strong tape or glue. Students can then decorate the haunted house with poster paints, construction paper, and other art materials to make it look spooky. To stabilize the puppet theater, place a paperweight or heavy stone on the bottom edge when you stand it on a table.

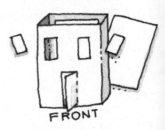

To make a "teeny tiny ghost" to haunt the house, children can crumple a tissue and stuff it inside another tissue, then tie the tissues around their finger. They may want to brainstorm ways to make other haunted characters, such as cats and bats. The ghost and other puppets can peer through the door and windows of the haunted-house theater as children perform a dramatic reading of the poem, complete with eerie music and sound effects.

Little Adventures: What would it be like to be "no bigger than a mouse, at most"? Invite children to create a chart of good and bad things about being teeny tiny. Extend the activity by asking students to write stories about the adventures they might have if they were mouse-size.

Teeny Tiny Ghost

A teeny tiny ghost
no bigger than a mouse,
at most,
lived in a great big house.

It's hard to haunt
a great big house
when you're a teeny tiny ghost
no bigger than a mouse,
at most.

He did what he could do.

So every dark and stormy night—
the kind that shakes a house with fright—
if you stood still and listened right,
you'd hear a
teeny
tiny
BOO!

—Lilian Moore

November

Something Told the Wild Geese

Poetry Pointers

The poem beautifully evokes the seasonal rhythms and the mystery of animal migration. However, it does contain some sophisticated language that you may want to preview with students; *luster-glossed*, *sagging*, *steamed*, *amber*, and *stiffened* are some of the words with which children may not be familiar. After reading the poem, ask children what they think is happening. What time of year is it? Why are the geese flying away? Encourage children to point out words and phrases in the poem that support their answers.

Inspirations

A Change of Seasons: The sight of migrating flocks of geese is a sign of winter's approach in cooler regions. As a class, brainstorm other signs of the seasonal change from autumn to winter, such as bare trees, cooler temperatures, frost in the morning, seeing clouds of breath, people wearing heavier clothing, and so on. Ask children to illustrate these changes on squares of white paper. Then glue their pictures to larger squares of construction paper in various colors. Staple the squares to a bulletin board or tape to a wall or door to create a cozy class quilt titled "Winter's on Its Way."

Feed the Birds: Discuss bird migration. Explain that not all birds migrate and that food can be hard to find for those that stick around. Make feeders to help non migratory birds through this difficult season. Provide each child with a pinecone and a piece of string. Help children tie the string to the top of the pinecone, knotting the ends together to form a loop. Using plastic knives, children can spread peanut butter on the pinecone. Next, roll the pinecones in cornmeal and then in birdseed. Hang the pinecones in shrubbery or trees. Arrange for children to observe the feeders daily, recording what they see in their science journals. Use a field guide designed for young bird-watchers to help children identify birds and find out more about them.

Something Told the Wild Geese

Something told the wild geese
   It was time to go.
Though the fields lay golden
   Something whispered—"Snow."
Leaves were green and stirring,
   Berries, luster-glossed,
But beneath warm feathers
   Something cautioned—"Frost."
All the sagging orchards
   Steamed with amber spice,
But each wild breast stiffened
   At remembered ice.
Something told the wild geese
   It was time to fly—
Summer sun was on their wings,
   Winter in their cry.

—Rachel Field

Colors Crackle, Colors Roar

Poetry Pointers

Pat Mora is a Latina poet who peppers her poetry with Spanish words and phrases. Before you use the glossary to translate the Spanish words in the poem, see if children can use context clues to figure out their meaning. Mora employs an array of poetic techniques to help the reader experience the energy and drama of color. Here are two to focus on:

✷ *Synesthesia* is the act of experiencing one sense—in this case, sight—through that of another—in this case, hearing. While the term isn't necessary for young children to know, you may want to draw their attention to this poetic device by asking, "Which of the five senses does the poet use to talk about colors?" Once students identify that sense as hearing, ask them to point out all the words that suggest sound, such as *crackle, roar, shout, clickety-clicks, sizzles, sings,* and so on. Underline these words in the poem.

✷ *Onomatopoeia* is the formation of words that imitate the sound they stand for, such as *clickety-click, sizzles,* and *coo-coo-coos* from the poem. When you read the poem, exaggerate these sounds to help bring the poem to life. Students may enjoy naming other onomatopoeiac words they know, such as *buzz, chirp, ding-dong,* and so on.

Inspirations

Pocket Chart Matchup: Just about every line of the poem suggests an animal, person, or object that is associated with a particular color. Some are specifically named while others are only suggested. Draw or cut out pictures of the following items and mount them on index cards: red balloon, brown stick, yellow flame, green leaf, a white piece of chalk writing on a chalkboard, gray kitten, silver bell, blue bird, purple storm cloud, gold tuba, orange tiger. Next, write the lines of the poem on oak-tag strips and put them in a pocket chart. Display the picture cards on the pocket chart as well, in no particular order. Reread the poem aloud. Pause after each line and invite volunteers to choose the picture card that best matches it.

A Splash of Color: November is often a gray month. Students can make roaring, crackling color collages to brighten the season. Divide children into small groups. Each group should pick one of the colors named in the poem, then hunt through magazines for images depicting their chosen color. They can use the pictures to create monochromatic collages on poster board. At the top of each collage, children may copy the line from the poem that corresponds with their color, for example, "Red shouts a loud, balloon-round sound."

Colors Crackle, Colors Roar

Red shouts a loud, balloon-round sound.
Black crackles like noisy grackles.*
Café clickety-clicks its wooden sticks.
Yellow sparks and sizzles, tzz-tzz.
White sings, Ay, her high, light note.
Verde rustles leaf secrets, swhish, swhish.
Gris whis-whis-whispers its kitten whiskers.
Silver ting-ting-a-ling jingles.
Azul coo-coo-coos like pajaritos do.
Purple thunders and rum-rum-rumbles.
Oro blares, a brassy, brass tuba.
Orange growls its striped, rolled roar.
Colors Crackle. Colors Roar.

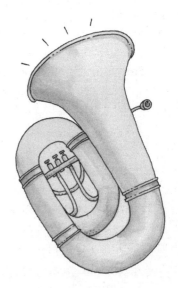

—Pat Mora

Glossary	
Café (kah-FEH): brown	Azul (ah-ZUHL): blue
Verde (VER-deh): green	Pajaritos (pah-hah-REE-toce): little birds
Gris (GREECE): gray	Oro (OH-roh): gold

* Grackle is a type of blackbird with shiny feathers.

What If . . .

Poetry Pointers

"What If..." is a fun way to commemorate National Children's Book Week, which falls annually during the third week of November. Ask students to hunt for rhyming words in the poem. As they search, they'll discover that most of the rhyming words fall within the lines rather than at the ends of lines. Ask children what's different about the second verse (there are no rhymes at all). Can students find a naming word—or noun—that the poet turned into an action word—or verb? (*dinosauring*) Invite students to make up a definition for the word *dinosauring*.

Inspirations

Ready! Set! Read!: Children can make dinosaur bookmarks using the template on the reproducible on page 114. Encourage students to read, or have someone read to them, as many books as possible during the week. Each morning, tally the total number of books read the previous day. At the end of Book Week, create a graph comparing daily totals and calculate the grand total of books read.

What If: Anything is possible in a book—or a poem. Children may enjoy using this selection as a model for writing their own "What If..." poems. Suggest that students think of another animal (butterfly, penguin, monkey) or character (pirate, clown, acrobat) that comes to life, steps out of a book, and overruns the classroom. Children may or may not want to include rhymes in their poems. To help them frame the poem, they can begin and end it as Isabel Joshlin Glaser does, for example:

What if...
You opened a book
About rabbits
And one hopped out
then another and another
and they hopped on your desk
and they hopped on your head
and one spilled juice on your homework
and one fell asleep on your spelling book
and one asked for a cookie

What if...
You tried to push them
Back inside
But they kept tromping
Off the pages instead?
Would you close the covers?

What If . . .

What if . . .
   You opened a book
   About dinosaurs
And one stumbled out
And another and another
   And more and more pour
Until the whole place
Is bumbling and rumbling
And groaning and moaning
   And snoring and roaring
And dinosauring?

What if . . .
   You tried to push them
   Back inside
But they kept tromping
Off the pages instead?
   Would you close the covers?

—Isabel Joshlin Glaser

Thanksgiving

Poetry Pointers

Tell students that poets use their five senses to help us see the world as they do. This poem offers a veritable cornucopia of sense imagery. Ask children to "listen" to the poem with all their senses: What do they hear, see, taste, and touch? Can they identify the one sense that the poet does not address in the poem? (the sense of smell)

Inspirations

A Sense of Thanks: Create a chart with five headings: See, Hear, Smell, Touch, Taste. Children can then generate a list of things they are thankful for, categorizing the items by the sensory heading each falls under. Students may enjoy writing a new stanza for the poem that focuses on the sense of smell. Suggest that they begin the stanza, "Thank you for all my nose can smell..." and incorporate the things they listed on the chart under this heading.

Spell It Out: In honor of the holiday, write a collaborative acrostic poem. Start by writing the word "THANKSGIVING" vertically on a sheet of chart paper. Each line of the poem should begin with one of the letters in the word. You may want to begin the poem the way Ivy Eastwick does: "Thank you for..." Invite contributions from the class by asking, "What are you thankful for that begins with the letter H?" Write down any letter-appropriate responses, such as "Happy days at the beach"; "Hippos in the zoo"; "Hair on my head"; and so on. Use the poem as the center of a holiday bulletin-board display by cutting out the letters in "THANKSGIVING" from red, gold, brown, and orange construction paper. Staple the letters to the bulletin board in a column. Transfer each line of your class poem to sentence strips, and staple these after the appropriate letters on the board. Surround the poem with student artwork depicting the poem's imagery.

Thanksgiving

Thank You
  for all my hands can hold—
    apples red,
     and melons gold,
      yellow corn
       both ripe and sweet,
       peas and beans
        so good to eat!

Thank You
  for all my eyes can see—
    lovely sunlight,
     field and tree,
      white cloud-boats
       in sea-deep sky,
       soaring bird
        and butterfly.

Thank You
  for all my ears can hear—
    birds' song echoing
     far and near,
      songs of little
       stream, big sea,
       cricket, bullfrog,
        duck and bee!

           —Ivy O. Eastwick

December

First Snowflake

Poetry Pointers

This short verse is rich in poetic technique. Ask children to identify the two similes in the poem, that is, the items the poet compares a snowflake to (*dandelion down* and *a raindrop in her winter nightgown*). The second simile is an example of *personification*, giving human traits to nonliving things. Discuss how the poet uses both techniques to create pictures in our minds and how this adds to our enjoyment of the poem.

Inspirations

Water and Ice: The poet likens a snowflake to a raindrop in winter dress. Tell students that this isn't far from the truth—that, if it's cold enough, snow will form inside a cloud instead of rain. Conduct a simple experiment to help children grasp the connection between water and ice. Fill a cup halfway with water. Use a thermometer to measure the temperature. Record the temperature on a chart. Put the cup in the freezer for 30 minutes. Measure and record the temperature again. Repeat the process every 30 minutes—breaking the thin crust of ice that forms over the water with a dull knife—until it is no longer possible to insert the thermometer. Remove the cup from the freezer, and repeat the temperature measuring and charting process every 30 minutes as the ice melts. Create a graph showing the temperatures you recorded, and ask children to draw conclusions about temperature's role in freezing and melting.

Pattern Pairs: Use handmade paper snowflakes for a lesson on symmetry and patterns. If possible, show students some magnified images of snowflakes that reveal their beautiful designs. Using coffee cans, have children trace circles onto white paper and cut them out. Next, they need to fold and cut the circle as shown in the diagrams below. They can cut along one of the snowflake's fold lines, dividing the snowflake into two symmetrical halves. Now split the class into three groups, and situate each group in a different part of the classroom. Group members can place both halves of their snowflakes on the floor or a tabletop, mix them up, and take turns trying to match the symmetrical halves. Students will have to look closely at the patterns to make correct matches.

First Snowflake

Snowflake,
snowflake,
blowing into town
like one, last,
summer's-end
dandelion down,
or a cold little
raindrop
in her winter nightgown.

—N. M. Bodecker

In the Summer We Eat

Poetry Pointers

After reading the poem, ask your students who is speaking—whom does the "we" refer to? Encourage them to look for clues in the poem if they have trouble figuring out that bears are its subject. Ask: Who sleeps in dens? Who sleeps, or *hibernates*, during the winter months? You may want to explain to students that bears are not true hibernators, rather they are *dormant*—or inactive—during the winter. Bats, chipmunks, and many rodents are true hibernators, meaning their body temperatures drop and their breathing slows down. While bears are largely at rest and don't eat, they can become instantly alert when disturbed.

Inspirations

Seasonal Activities: Ask students to fold a sheet of paper into four equal parts. In the top part and bottom part of the left side of the page, they should copy the following phrases:

In the summer I _____.

In the winter I _____.

Ask students to complete each sentence with an activity they enjoy in the summer and winter, respectively. Children can draw pictures of themselves doing the activity in the empty squares next to each sentence. Bind the pages into a class book about summer and winter activities.

The Bear Facts: Create a reading corner that includes lots of nonfiction books about bears. Provide each child with a copy of the reproducible bear paw-print pattern on page 115. Children can then write facts they discover about bears on the paw-print patterns. Tape the paw prints in a meandering line along a classroom wall to create a "trail" of bear facts.

In the Summer We Eat

In the summer we eat,
in the winter we don't;
In the summer we'll play,
in the winter we won't.
All winter we sleep, each curled in a ball
As soon as the snowflakes start to fall.
But in spring we each come out of our den
And start to eat all over again.

—Zhenya Gay

Hanukkah Treats • A Secret • Kwanzaa

Poetry Pointers

You may want to share some of this background information with students after reading these three holiday poems:

✳ **Christmas**, a Christian holiday, falls annually on December 25 and celebrates the birth of Jesus. The custom of decorating pine trees dates back to the 8th century. Legend holds that the custom was originated by a German monk.

✳ **Hanukkah**, a Jewish holiday beginning the 25th day of the Hebrew month of Kislev, commemorates the triumph of the Maccabees over the army of the Syrian king, Antiochus IV. Among Hanukkah traditions is the lighting of the menorah, which symbolizes the miracle of the one-day supply of oil that burned for eight days when the victorious Maccabees rededicated the temple that had been seized by Antiochus. It has been said that the oil in which potato latkes are cooked represents the miracle of the long-burning menorah oil.

✳ A celebration of African American heritage, **Kwanzaa** begins on December 26 and ends on January 1. During the holiday, families reflect on seven Kwanzaa principles: unity, purpose, creativity, faith, self-determination, collective work and responsibility, and cooperative economics. During a special ceremony, symbolic items are placed on a straw mat. Among the items are a bowl of fruit and vegetables, which symbolize the harvest, and ears of corn, which represent children and the future.

Inspirations

It's a Tradition: Use the poems as a springboard for discussing the winter holidays. Set aside time for a holiday symbol show-and-tell. Children can then bring in and talk about the significance of an object that represents a part of their family's holiday traditions; for example, a menorah or *dreidel* (a top that's a traditional Hanukkah game), a Christmas stocking or favorite ornament, a *mkeka* (straw mat used in a special Kwanzaa ceremony) or *kinara* (candleholder in which candles representing the seven Kwanzaa principles are placed).

Now We're Cookin': Food is an important part of holiday traditions. Ask children to bring from home a favorite recipe that is part of their family celebrations this season. Use the recipes to create a class cookbook. For a special treat, invite family volunteers in to prepare traditional holiday foods for a winter festival.

Hanukkah Treats

Come, children, come,
    Come quick as you can.
Latkes are sizzling
    Hot in the pan.
Soon they'll be browning,
    Ready to eat.
Come, children, come
    For Hanukkah's treat.

Come, children, come,
    Come merry and bright.
Presents are waiting,
    Hidden from sight—
Secrets in wrappings.
    Need I repeat?
Come, children, come
    For Hanukkah's treat.

      —Elbee Jay

A Secret

Do you know why the pine trees
    Stand so straight and tall,
Spread their branches thick and fine,
    And never stoop at all?

It really is a secret
    Which the North Wind told to me:
Every pine tree hopes some day
    To be a Christmas tree.

—Laura Alice Boyd

Kwanzaa

Where there is Kwanzaa
    there is corn:

    An ear of corn
    for every child;

    Where there is corn
    there is a dream,

    a dream of growth
    wondrous and wild;

    a dream of strength,
    of unity

    for generations
    yet unborn.

    Where there is dreaming
    there is child.

Where there is Kwanzaa
    there is corn.

    —Myra Cohn Livingston

How to Talk to Your Snowman

Poetry Pointers

Read the poem aloud to children, but leave out the last word, *bake*. Ask children to guess what the missing word might be, using both logic and rhyme as clues. You may want to offer students some guidance by pointing out that the word would be the opposite of a cold-weather word and that it would rhyme with *shake*. Point out the author's use of *alliteration*, or repetition of the initial consonant sound in lines 5 and 7. (*blizzard* and *blow; say, shiver,* and *shake*)

Inspirations

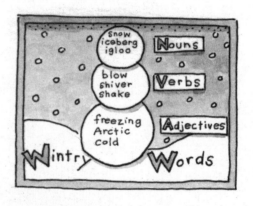

Wintry Words: Create a winter word bank that students can use as reference for seasonally themed writing activities. Ask children to identify all the words in the poem that suggest winter and cold weather. They can then brainstorm other wintry words to add to the list. Create an icy-blue, snow-swept landscape on which to display all the words. First, cover a bulletin board with light-blue construction paper. Next, mix 3 tablespoons salt with a 1/4 cup water. Brush the mixture onto the paper and allow to dry. Make a large snowman shape from white paper. The snowman should consist of three "snowballs." Ask children to categorize the words they came up with by part of speech: naming words (nouns), describing words (adjectives), and action words (verbs). Create corresponding labels for each of the "snowballs" that make the snowman's shape, and list the words accordingly.

Follow the Directions: "How to Talk to Your Snowman" is a poem of instruction: It makes forceful statements, telling the reader what to do. Children may enjoy using the poem as a model for writing their own poems of instruction. Encourage students to use their imaginations, as the poet did, to pick a "how-to" topic for their poems. Here are a few ideas to get them started:

    How to talk like the rain
    How to make friends with a mouse
    How to fly like a bird
    How to catch a baby dragon
    How to make a rainbow

How to Talk to Your Snowman

Use words that are pleasing,
Like: freezing
And snow,
Iceberg and igloo
And blizzard and blow,
Try: Arctic, Antarctic,
Say: shiver and shake,
But whatever you never say,
Never say: bake.

—Beverly McLoughland

January

Beginning a New Year Means

Poetry Pointers

Ask children how this poem is different from some of the others you may have shared with them from this book. Can they find any rhymes in the poem? Remind students that not all poems need to rhyme, and this is an example of one that does not. Also interesting about this poem is the fact that the title really reads as its first line. Encourage students to look closely at the images that form the first and second stanzas. What three "old" things does the poet mention in the first stanza? Can students find their "new" counterparts in the second stanza? *(dirty clothes/clean clothes, scribbled pages/white pages, old snow/fresh snow)*

Inspirations

Identifying Opposites: The structure of the poem lends itself well to a sequencing activity and lesson on opposites. A pocket chart works great for this activity. Begin by copying each of the three images in the first stanza on separate strips of oak tag, as shown at right. Repeat with the second stanza. Place the images of the first stanza, in order, on the left side of a pocket chart. Invite volunteers to put the images in the second stanza of the poem in order on the right side of the pocket chart. Each line in the first stanza should be matched with the line that is its opposite. Extend this activity by brainstorming a list of other old/new things that can be added to the first and second stanzas.

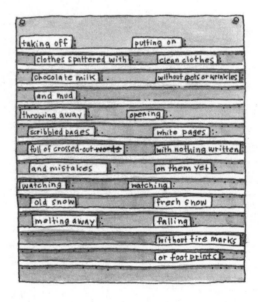

Month by Month: What better time to review the order of the months of the year than at the beginning of a new one? Write the name of each month in black marker on different color pieces of construction paper. Scramble the pages up and attach them to a line with clothespins. Invite students to put the months of the year in the proper order, beginning with January. Children may enjoy making calendars for the new year, perhaps using a seasonal poem to introduce each month.

Beginning a New Year Means

taking off
    clothes spattered with
    chocolate milk
    and mud
throwing away
    scribbled pages
    full of crossed out ~~words~~
    and mistakes
watching
    old snow
    melting away

putting on
    clean clothes
    without spots or wrinkles
opening
    white pages
    with nothing written
    on them yet
watching
    fresh snow
    falling
    without tiremarks
    or footprints

—Ruth Whitman

Perhaps

Poetry Pointers

Ask children to listen for all the words that describe how penguins move. (*diving, splashing, leaping, dashing*) Can children think of other colorful words to describe penguins playing in the water? In what ways can we describe the way penguins move on land?

Inspirations

Same and Different: Share a variety of books about penguins with your students. *Penguins!* by Gail Gibbons (Holiday House, 1998) and *Penguins at Home* by Bruce McMillan (Houghton Mifflin, 1993) are two good nonfiction titles to share with young readers. After students learn more about penguins, work together as a class to create a Venn diagram that illustrates how penguins are similar to and different from another type of bird they are familiar with, such as a robin or a chicken.

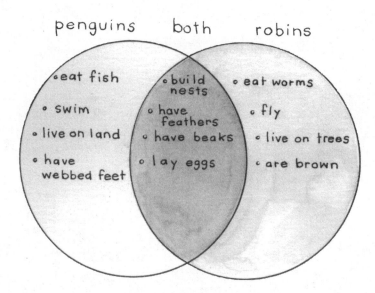

Animal Charades: While penguins are graceful swimmers, they're known for their awkward, waddling walk on land. Invite children to imitate the penguins' comical way of walking. Ask students to name other animals that move in distinctive ways. Children may enjoy playing a game of animal charades, taking turns imitating how various animals move. Invite their classmates to guess which animal they are. As a language arts enrichment, brainstorm a list of words that describe the myriad ways animals get around—*fly, hop, scurry, crawl, creep, slither, wiggle, gallop, swim, flutter,* and so on.

Perhaps

All day long the penguins play
in the cold Antarctic sea—
diving
     splashing
leaping
     dashing
in slippery, flippery glee.
While other birds chase blue-sky dreams
the sea to penguins sings—
perhaps they aren't birds at all
but fish with feet and wings.

               —Maxwell Higgins

Dreams

Poetry Pointers

In the poem, Langston Hughes uses two striking *metaphors* to convey what it feels like to lose one's dreams. Before reading the poem, be sure students understand the meaning of the word *barren*, since it's crucial to grasping the emotional content of the second metaphor. Then ask students to close their eyes as you read the poem. After they open their eyes again, ask them to describe the pictures they saw in their heads. How did those pictures make them feel? What is the poem comparing the picture of the broken-winged bird and the barren field to? *(lost dreams)*

Inspirations

Dream Keepers: Use the poem as a way to commemorate the life of Martin Luther King Jr., who shared his dream for a better world and worked to make it come true. King's birthday, January 15, is celebrated annually as a national holiday on the third Monday in January. Read aloud King's famous "I Have a Dream" speech. Then, to honor King, invite children to write their own dreams for making the world a better place. Allow time for children to share their dreams with the class. Discuss steps they can take to help make their dreams come true.

Practicing Metaphor: Hughes compares something you can't see or touch or measure (dreams) with something you can see and touch (a bird, a field), making an abstract idea very concrete and real. This adds to our understanding of the concept of dreams. Write a list of feelings or other "big idea" words on the board. Invite children to write a metaphor, or comparison, that helps us understand what the word means. Tell students that the comparison should paint a picture with words by telling about something we can see, smell, hear, touch, or taste. For example: Happiness is a field of dancing sunflowers. In addition to words that name feelings, words such as *silence, hope,* and *friendship* are rich with possibilities, as are the names of the four seasons.

Dreams

Hold fast to dreams
For if dreams die
Life is a broken-winged bird
That cannot fly.

Hold fast to dreams
For when dreams go
Life is a barren field
Frozen with snow.

　　　—Langston Hughes

Chinese New Year

Poetry Pointers

Before reading the poem, provide children with some background information about the holiday. Chinese New Year falls on the first day of the new moon, usually between January 21 and February 20. To celebrate the holiday, people give thanks for the preceding year and get ready for the new one. As you read the poem aloud, ask students to listen for a phrase that's repeated. Then draw their attention to the last line of each stanza. Point out that the repeated language provides a kind of glue that holds the stanzas of the poem together.

Inspirations

New Year Traditions: The poem highlights many of the traditions that are part of Chinese New Year celebrations. Invite someone who celebrates the holiday to read the poem with your class, pausing to explain the traditions, customs, and symbols that the poem touches upon. Children may also enjoy learning about the Chinese Zodiac, and identifying the animals and characteristics that match their year of birth. Be sure your class wishes your visitor *Gung Hay Fat Choy*— "Happy New Year!"

Catch Me If You Can!: The dragon is the Chinese symbol of strength and goodness. An elaborately decorated dragon dancing through the streets is the highlight of Chinese New Year parades. Chuo Tung Wek, or "Catching the Dragon's Tail," is a traditional game played by children in China. Your students can play the game by following the instructions below. Be sure to choose a wide-open space for this activity, such as a gymnasium or playing field:

1. Form a long line by placing your hands on the shoulders of the person in front of you. The first person in the line is the dragon's head; the last person is the very end of the dragon's tail.

2. To start the game, everyone shouts together "em, er, san, ko!" ("one, two, three go!"). Then the "head" tries to catch the "tail." The line of children must twist and turn to keep the head from catching the tail.

3. If someone lets go and breaks the line, he or she leaves the game, and the pieces of the dragon join together again.

4. When the head catches the tail, the head leaves his or her place at the front of the line and becomes the end of the tail. The new child at the front of the line then becomes the dragon's head and the game continues.

Chinese New Year

Flowers and Nin Wah,
Tangerines, oranges,
Wealth and good fortune
    and luck to us all!

Midnight will bring us
Red envelopes, Lai-See,
Filled with some money
    and riches for all!

Time for remembering
Grandparents, parents,
Neighbors and friends:
    with fine gifts for them all!

We will be offered
A tray of togetherness,
Seeds, candied coconut,
    sweetmeats for all!

Days of the Dragon Play,
Nights filled with singing,
Then comes Ten Chieh
    with lanterns for all!

Soon the parade starts—
With loud firecrackers!—
The dragon is here!—
    Happy New Year to all!

    —Myra Cohn Livingston

Glossary
Nin Wah: pictures
Lai-See: good-luck money
Ten Chieh: the Feast of the Lanterns, which, along with a parade, traditionally ends the New Year celebration

February

Groundhog Day

Poetry Pointers

Before reading the poem, discuss the folklore behind Groundhog Day, which falls annually on February 2. According to folk wisdom, if the groundhog sees its shadow when it emerges from its burrow, winter will last another six weeks. If it fails to see its shadow, myth holds that there will be an early spring. Ask children to look for examples of *alliteration* in the poem, such as *green* and *grassy* in lines 5 and 6, and *nicely newly nibbly* in line 7.

Inspirations

Sweet Dreams: Here's a dreamy mural that will see your class through to spring. First review the terms *hibernation* and *dormancy* with students. Then distribute nature magazines and ask children to cut out pictures of animals that hibernate during winter (bats, chipmunks, groundhogs, dormice, frogs) and those who are dormant (bears, skunks). Tape the pictures along the bottom edge of a sheet of craft paper, leaving lots of space between the animals. Above each animal's head, draw a dream bubble. In the bubbles, children can draw what the animals might be dreaming of during their long winter sleep. The children can finish the mural by drawing appropriate scenery around the animals, such as bare trees and frozen ponds and streams.

Shadow Watchers: What makes a shadow? Explain that when light hits some objects, it cannot pass through and the object casts a shadow. But not all objects are light blockers, or shadow casters. Divide children into groups and provide each group with the following items: tissue paper, a small plastic bag, waxed paper, cardboard, black construction paper, a plastic lid, and a clear plastic bottle. In their science journals, have students predict whether or not each object will cast a shadow when they shine a light on it. Then provide each group with a flashlight, darken the room, and have students test their predictions. Encourage children to pay particular attention to whether the shadows cast by different objects are distinct or faint. Introduce students to the terms *opaque, translucent,* and *transparent.* Have them categorize the items accordingly.

Groundhog Day

Groundhog sleeps
All winter
Snug in his fur,
Dreams
Green dreams of
Grassy shoots,
Of nicely newly nibbly
Roots—
Ah, he starts to
Stir.
With drowsy
Stare
Looks from his burrow
Out on fields of
Snow.
What's there!
Oh no.
His shadow. Oh,
How sad!
Six more
Wintry
Weeks
To go.

—Lilian Moore

A Million Valentines

Poetry Pointers

Point out to children that the poet uses exaggeration to tell how much he loves his valentine. Show the students how to write the large numbers in the poem by adding zeros: 100; 1,000; 1,000,000; and 1,000,000,000,000. Write the poem on a piece of chart paper, then write the numeral form for each of the numbers in the poem on a self-sticking note. Distribute the numerals to children. Reread the poem, pausing after each number. Students with the corresponding numerals should then step forward and place the self-sticking note over the number word it matches.

Inspirations

How Much Is a Hundred?: A "million million" are a lot of valentines to make, but your students may be able to handle 100! Divide children into small groups. Then, as a class, calculate how many valentines each group will have to create to reach 100. Provide students with a variety of art materials and let them get to work. Punch a hole through the top of each valentine, and knot a string through it to create a loop for hanging. To help students visualize the number 100, hang the valentines from pushpins on a bulletin board. Then spread all that love around by distributing the valentines to school staff and volunteers, residents at a nursing home, or patients at a children's hospital.

Sweetheart Math: The brightly colored candy conversation hearts that abound in February make excellent math manipulatives that can form the basis for estimation, counting, classifying, and graphing activities. Following are a few activities to try. (You may want to keep extra candy hearts on hand for nibbling so that students won't be tempted to eat the manipulatives!)

1. Fill a class jar with the hearts, and estimate how many are in it.

2. Use a counting mat to skip-count 100 hearts by twos, fives, and tens.

3. Sort the hearts by color and/or printed message. Graph the results.

4. Create valentine-themed word problems, and use the hearts as manipulatives to solve them. For example, "Maura bought a box of 24 valentines and she gave 16 away. How many were left over?"

A Million Valentines

I'll cut a Valentine
Just for you.
I'll cut out one,
I'll cut out two,
I'll cut out three,
I'll cut out four,
I'll cut out five—
Or maybe more.
I'll cut a hundred,
A thousand too.
I'll cut a million
Just for you.
A million million
Are too few
To say how much
I love you!

—Robert Heidbreder

Penny Problem

Poetry Pointers

Here's a poem to help commemorate Presidents' Day, which is celebrated annually on the third Monday in February. Before reading the poem, ask children if they know who is pictured on the penny. (Abraham Lincoln) What things do they know about Lincoln? List what they say on chart paper. After reading the poem, you may want to discuss the "big dreams" Lincoln had for our country in greater depth by putting them in the historical context of slavery, the secession of the southern states, and the Civil War. In the poem, the word *big* is used both literally and figuratively. Draw students' attention to this duel meaning by asking them to compare the use of *big* in the first and second stanzas. In the first stanza, *big* refers to Lincoln's physical size; in the second, it means "important."

Inspirations

Face Value: Review with students which presidents are on different coins (Alexander Hamilton is on the nickel; Dwight Eisenhower is on the dime; George Washington is on the quarter). On index cards, write some presidential problems for students to solve, such as: "One Eisenhower plus one Hamilton plus three Lincolns equals what amount?" Have coins on hand to help children with the calculations.

Lifelines: Create time lines illustrating the lives of some of our nation's greatest leaders in honor of Presidents' Day. Divide children into groups and have each group pick a different president. Students can then research the life of their chosen president, write date-specific facts on index cards, and hang them in sequential order on a clothesline. Children may want to intersperse the fact cards with picture cards to make their time lines visually interesting.

Penny Problem

Abe Lincoln was a BIG man—
a GIANT in every way—
with GREAT LONG LEGS
and a GREAT TALL HAT
and a GREAT BIG HEART, they say.

And he dreamed BIG DREAMS for our country:
that one day, all people would be FREE
that we'd be one STRONG, UNITED nation,
that we'd live in PEACE and HARMONY.

But when I look at Abe Lincoln on a penny
a leader who in history stands TALL,
I wonder just how it is they managed
to fit him on a coin

        so

          small.

            —Maxwell Higgins

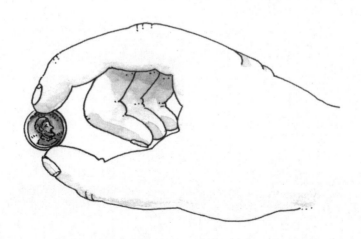

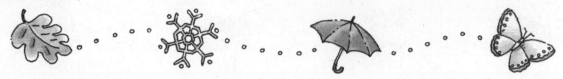

But Then

Poetry Pointers

Before reading the poem to children, cover up the word *tooth* in lines 1 and 9. Ask students to guess what the poet is writing about. By the last line, students will probably realize that the topic is teeth. Remind them that February is Dental Health Month. Use the poem to launch a discussion about teeth and how to take care of them.

Inspirations

Tooth Count: Chances are, many of your students can relate to the speaker in the poem and have lost one or more of their "baby teeth," which are known as *deciduous teeth*. Deciduous teeth start to fall out when children are about six years old. They are replaced by *secondary teeth*, which are permanent. Children can use the tooth patterns on the reproducible on page 116 to make a picture graph showing how many teeth each member of the class has lost. For a fun follow-up to this activity, share the book *Throw Your Tooth on the Roof* by Selby B. Beeler (Houghton Mifflin, 1998), which highlights tooth-fairy traditions around the world.

Keep' em Clean: In honor of Dental Health Month, children may enjoy creating posters that promote good dental hygiene. Begin by brainstorming different things we can do to help keep our teeth healthy, for example, brushing at least twice a day, avoiding sugary foods and drinks, choosing tooth-healthy snacks such as apples and cheese, and visiting the dentist regularly. Students can work on the posters in small groups, then display their finished work around the school as public-service announcements.

But Then

A tooth fell out
and left a space
so big my tongue
can touch my FACE.

And every time
I smile, I show
a space where some-
thing used to grow.

I miss my tooth,
as you may guess,
but then—I have to
brush one less.

—Aileen Fisher

March

Invitation to the Wind

Poetry Pointers

The short lines and repetition of the word *dance* give this poem a strong beat. Read it aloud, hitting the action words forcefully to suggest the waves of rhythm that carry the poem much like gusts of wind. Ask children to identify all the action words, and highlight them with a marker.

Inspirations

Whirl with the Wind: The strong rhythm of the poem lends itself readily to interpretation through movement. Practice reading the poem together as a class several times so students can internalize its rhythm. Then find some open space—a gymnasium or, even better, a field on a windy day—and allow children time to invent and practice their own "wind dances." Suggest that children hold out their arms in front of them, with hands joined together as if they're encircling and dancing with the wind. Divide the class in half. One group can perform a choral reading of the poem while the other group performs its "wind dance." Then groups can switch roles.

When the Wind Blows: On the next windy day, ask children to go outside or observe from the window signs that the wind is blowing. Suggest that students record their observations in their science journals. Can they tell by looking outside how hard the wind is blowing? Assist students in making a weather instrument for just that purpose: a wind sock. Begin by providing each child with a strip of cardboard that is about 1½ feet long. Children can then decorate the cardboard strip with crayons, glitter, and other art materials. Staple the ends of the cardboard strip together to form a ring. Next, staple several long strips of colorful crepe paper around the ring. Punch holes in the top of the ring and loop a piece of string through it. If possible, hang the wind socks outside your classroom window or in another outdoor spot where students can readily observe them on windy days. Compare the way the streamers move depending on the strength of the wind.

Invitation to the Wind

Dance
with me
now
in the Springlight
dance
with me under the sky.
Dance
on
your
tiptoes and turn me and
whirl me and lift me
and teach me to fly!
Carry me
on your wild shoulders
I'll
catch all the petals
that spill!
Dance with me,
Wind,
like
you
dance
with the kites
Like you dance with those kites
on the hill!

—Barbara Juster Esbensen

The Fairies

Poetry Pointers

This magical poem sets just the right tone for commemorating St. Patrick's Day, which falls on March 17. You may want to preview some of the vocabulary in the poem to enhance students' understanding of it. *Forest glen, brook, nook, jay, thistle, spike,* and *thistledown* are some of the words with which students may be unfamiliar. Patricia Hubbell's poem is rich in action and imagery. Point out that in the first line of the poem, she directs the reader to "See the fairies dancing," then provides a string of images—pictures painted with words—to help us do just that. Linger on some of the vivid images in the poem to give children time to envision the lively, leaping fairies skipping across a duck's back, jumping over a jay, swinging on a thistle. Ask what these images suggest about the fairies' size.

Inspirations

A Puppet Performance: How do children see the fairies in their mind's eye? Invite each child to draw a picture of a fairy. Students can use their pictures to create stick puppets by gluing each drawing to a piece of oak tag, cutting out the shape, and attaching it to a craft stick using strong tape. Next, create a mural depicting a lush forest scene. Be sure students include in the mural some of the details mentioned in the poem, such as a stone wall, a brook, a duck, a jay, and thistle. Groups of children will enjoy taking turns reading the poem as other students dramatize the fairies' actions by moving the stick puppets against the forest backdrop.

Luck of the Irish: Here's a great way to celebrate St. Patrick's Day, anticipate the arrival of spring, and grow a little luck: Using the patterns on the reproducible on page 117, help children trace a shamrock shape onto a flat, dry sponge. Cut the shamrock shapes out. Soak the sponges in water, wringing them out slightly (sponges should be very damp, but not dripping wet). Sprinkle the sponges generously with grass seeds and place on pieces of waxed paper in a cool, dark place until the seeds sprout. Place the sprouted sponges on a sunny windowsill and watch your luck start to grow! Students can record observations about the growing process in their science journals. Be sure to keep the sponges moist by watering frequently.

The Fairies

See the fairies dancing in
    the misty meadow hay,
Leaping on the stone wall, up and away.
One little, two little, seven little men,
Dancing in the shadows of the forest glen,
Down past the oak tree
Down past the brook
Dancing through the valley to
    the fairies' nook.
Skip across a duck's back
Jump across a jay
Leap fairies, leap fairies, leap and away;
Up a hairy thistle
Swinging on the spike
Jump into the thistledown
Sleep all night!

—Patricia Hubbell

Riddle

Poetry Pointers

Pause after you read line 7 and allow children to guess the answer to the riddle before proceeding. Did students guess correctly? How do they feel on the first warm, sunny day of spring? Talk about the way the position of the words in the last eight lines of the poem suggests movement, such as *bouncing, hopping, skipping,* or *jumping.* Do they think the poet feels the way they do about spring?

Inspirations

Discovery Walk: Whether you live in a city, a suburb, or the country, there are sure to be signs that spring is in the air. Take the children on a walk around the school grounds or in a park. Ask them to try to find signs of spring's arrival. Encourage them to use all their senses (except, for safety reasons, taste). Be sure students take along their science journals to record notes and sketches. Back in the classroom, create a chart that indicates which senses children used to detect each "sign of spring," for example, they may see and hear a robin; they may see and feel a pussy willow; they may see and smell cherry blossoms; and so on.

That Zingy, Swingy Season: Hubbell's whimsical language captures the light-hearted joy many people feel upon the arrival of spring. Draw students' attention to the language Hubbell uses in lines 10 to 14. What do they notice about these words? (They all rhyme and they all end in "y"; some are made-up words.) Explain to children that Hubbell is being playful with language by turning some action words into describing words. As a class, brainstorm a list of adjectives to describe spring. If students suggest nouns or verbs, ask if they can substitute a related describing word, either real or invented, i.e., instead of *bird,* they might list *chirpy* or *tweety; flowery* instead of *flower;* and so on. Use the templates on the reproducible on page 112 to trace butterfly shapes onto color construction paper. Write each word on a butterfly shape, cut the shapes out, and hang them on a bulletin board. Children can use this language-rich display as inspiration for writing their own fanciful spring poems.

Riddle

Who dances lightly through the world
in slippers mossy green?

Who covers trees with tiny leaves
where birds can hide unseen?

Who brings the flowers?
Who brings the showers?
Who brings the butterflies?

Of course, you know the answer—

That
    zingy
        wingy
            singy
                flingy
                    swingy
                        season
                            SPRING!

—Patricia Hubbell

Frog's Lullaby

Poetry Pointers

If children do not know what a polliwog is, explain that it is another name for a tadpole, or young frog. The poet uses playful language to create a silly song that echoes a tadpole's wiggly movement. *Alliteration* helps make the poem musical. Ask students to point out all the phrases that repeat the initial consonant sound, for example, *pretty polliwog* in line 1 and *wolly wiggle wog* in line 2.

Inspirations

Growing Up: Review the differences among mammals, reptiles, and amphibians. Explain to children that while mammal and reptile babies look like their parents, amphibians do not. They undergo a physical change called *metamorphosis*. After further investigating the process of metamorphosis with students, show them how to construct sequence books to illustrate the life cycle of a frog. Provide each student with a piece of white 8"-x-11" paper and have them follow these directions:

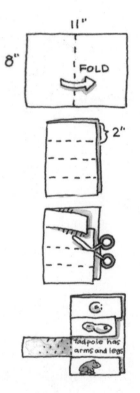

1. Fold the paper in half vertically.

2. Measure four 2" segments, as shown in the diagram. Draw a line to mark off each segment.

3. Cut along each line, being careful to cut only the top part of the folded page.

4. On top of each flap, draw pictures showing—in sequence— four stages in a frog's development, from egg to adult.

5. Under each flap, write a sentence describing what is happening in the corresponding picture.

Children can bring their books home to share with family members.

Look How You've Grown!: Do children look like they did when they were babies? Invite students to bring in pictures of themselves as babies or toddlers. Display the photographs on a bulletin board, and see if children can match each baby picture to the correct classmate. Help children create time lines that highlight important events in their own young lives, including the year they were born, when they took their first steps, said their first words, lost their first tooth, and so on. Children can consult with family members to help fill in the facts.

Frog's Lullaby

Sleep, my pretty polliwog,
Polly wolly wiggle wog

Polly wiggle waggle wog
Wiggle waggle woggle wog

Polly wolly wiggle waggle
Wiggle waggle woggle froggle

Sleep, my little wiggle head,
In your little water bed.

Sweet dreams, pretty polliwog.
When you wake, you'll be a frog.

—Charlotte Pomerantz

April

The Folk Who Live in Backward Town

Poetry Pointers

Here's a silly poem to commemorate that silliest of holidays: April Fools' Day, which falls annually on April 1 and kicks off National Humor Month. The custom of tricking people on the first day of April can be traced to Europe. Before the 16th century, the new year began on March 25. People celebrated the beginning of the new year for eight days. On the final day of the celebration, April 1, people visited one another and exchanged gifts. But then the calendar was changed, and January 1 became the start of the new year. However, some people continued the April 1 traditions, and they were called "April fools." After you read the poem, ask children to explain how the things the folks in "Backward Town" do differ from what's "normal."

Inspirations

The Land of Opposites: Ask children to keep a diary of their activities on a typical day, from waking in the morning to going to sleep at night. The following day, ask children to pretend they are residents of Backward Town. How might they do each activity in their diaries differently? For example, they might wake up at night and go to bed in the morning, or walk to school on their hands instead of their feet. Groups of students can incorporate their ideas into new diary entries, titled "A Day in the Life in Backward Town." Allow time for groups to share their wacky diaries.

Nutty News: In honor of April Fools' Day, create a newspaper that includes outlandish headlines, stories, and pictures about improbable events. Distribute the newspaper to other classes.

The Folk Who Live in Backward Town

The folk who live in Backward Town
Are inside out and upside down.
They wear their hats inside their heads
And go to sleep beneath their beds.
They only eat the apple peeling
And take their walks across the ceiling.

—Mary Ann Hoberman

Chatterbox, The Rain

Poetry Pointers

The poet uses the device of *personification*—assigning human traits to inanimate objects—to describe the rain. After reading the poem aloud to children, ask them if the rain really "talks." When the poet mentions the rain talking, what does she actually mean? (the sound the rain makes when it falls) Tell children that the poet brings the rain to life by giving it the human trait of speech. Another technique the poet employs is *onomatopoeia*, the use of words that suggest the sound they name, such as *buzz* or *rumble*. Ask students if they can find two examples of this in the poem. (*rattles* in line 6, *babbles* in line 7)

Inspirations

Wet-Weather Words: Children can work in small groups to make shape books that catalog the many things "Chatterbox, the Rain" has to say. Begin by providing each group with a copy of the raindrop-shaped template on the reproducible on page 118. Students can then trace the shape onto blue construction paper several times and cut out raindrop-shaped pages for their books. Next, group members can brainstorm a list of onomatopoeic words that echo the sound of rain falling, such as *pitter-pat, plip, plop, whoosh, splash,* and so on. To help spark children's thinking, suggest that they imagine the different sounds rain makes when it hits different objects (such as the windowpane or trash-can lid mentioned in the poem). Children can write their wet-weather words on the fronts and backs of the raindrop patterns. Stack the raindrops so that their edges line up, punch a hole through the top of the stack, and knot a piece of colorful yarn through the hole to tie the pages together. Students can title their books "Chatterbox, the Rain."

Measuring April's Showers: In many parts of the country, April is a rainy month. Talk about the adage "April showers bring May showers." Invite children to make a simple rain gauge to measure April's showers where they live. Using a permanent marker, indicate 1/2" increments on a piece of masking tape. Place the tape inside an empty coffee can so that its bottom edge touches the bottom of the can. Place the can outside in an open area. Then partially bury the can in the ground so that it won't blow away or get knocked over by a small animal. For the month of April, have students check the amount of rainfall in the can each day and chart their measurements. Don't forget to empty the can after measuring each rainfall. If possible, obtain the monthly rainfall totals for your area so far this year, and have children compare the numbers. Does April seem as rainy as its reputation suggests? Discuss why it might be useful for meteorologists to keep track of how much rain falls.

Chatterbox, The Rain

Bursting with news,
Chatterbox, the Rain,
Talks all day
To the windowpane,

To the trash can lid
Rattles on and on,
Babbles this and that
To the backyard lawn,

Chatterbox, the Rain,
Talks and talks all day,
And still has puddles
And puddles to say.

—Beverly McLoughland

Valentine for Earth

Poetry Pointers

This poet's lyrical tribute to our planet makes it a natural tie-in for Earth Day celebrations. Earth Day falls annually on April 22. Unusual about "Valentine for Earth" is the poet's decision to break stanzas two and three in mid-sentence. As you read the poem, pause as the stanza breaks indicate to allow young listeners' minds to linger over the poem's imagery. You may want to point out to children the use of the word *silver* as a verb in line 19 of the poem. Explain to students that poets try to use language in surprising ways to make a poem come alive.

Inspirations

Happy Earth Day to You: Instead of a birthday party, throw an Earth Day party, with our wonderful planet as the honoree. Invite students to make a colorful banner appropriate for the occasion. You may want to bake an Earth Day cake: a round cake decorated with blue and green tinted frosting so that it resembles Earth. Children can make Earth Day cards from recycled scraps of paper. Suggest that they address cards directly to Earth, and include a short message of thanks to our planet. Students also may enjoy composing new lyrics for "Happy Birthday (Earth Day) to You" to sing at the party as a special tribute.

Giving Back: Make a two-columned chart, with the heading "Gifts the Earth Gives Us" at the top of the left column, and "Gifts We Give the Earth" at the top of the right column. Reread the poem, and ask students to name all of the things the poet loves about the Earth. List these in the first column, then ask children to add their own ideas about what makes the Earth great. As a class, brainstorm gifts we can give back to our planet, for example, conserving water, recycling garbage, planting trees, and so on. List these things in the second column. Challenge students to put their ideas into action.

Valentine for Earth

Oh, it will be fine
To rocket through space
And see the reverse
Of the moon's dark face,

To travel to Saturn
Or Venus or Mars,
Or maybe discover
Some uncharted stars.

But do they have anything
Better than we?
Do you think, for instance,
They have a blue sea

For sailing and swimming?
Do the planets have hills
With raspberry thickets
Where a song sparrow fills

The summer with music?
And do they have snow
To silver the roads
Where the school buses go?

Oh, I'm all for rockets
And worlds cold or hot,
But I'm wild in love
With the planet we've got!

—Frances Frost

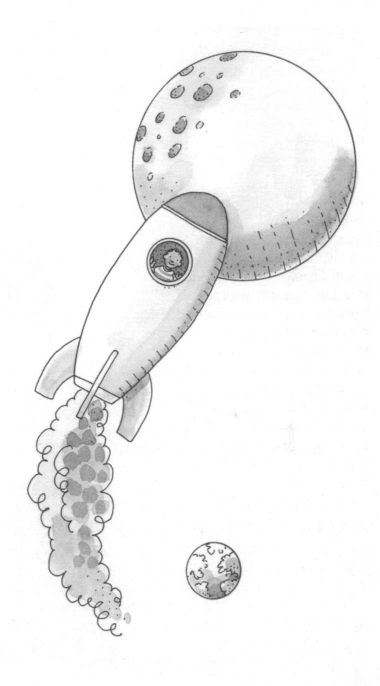

Who?

Poetry Pointers

Encourage children to guess the answer to this spring-themed riddle. You may want to make it clear to children that the poet is not really talking about a house, rather she is comparing some object in nature to a house; she is using a *metaphor*. Encourage students to think carefully about the clues: What kind of object holds something living inside it like a house does? Be sure that students understand that *frail* means "easy to break," then ask students to think about this clue as well. Once students figure out the "house" is an egg, they're sure to guess that the "who" in the poem's title is a chick or some other animal that hatches from an egg.

Inspirations

Hatch a Batch of Riddles: Students can research the kinds of animals that hatch from eggs as well as facts about them. Provide children with copies of the reproducibles on pages 119 and 120. Inside the egg shape of the reproducible on page 119, students should draw or paste a picture of an animal that hatches from an egg. Next, students should cut out the cracked egg shape on reproducible

page 120. They then need to cover the picture of the animal inside the first egg with the cracked-egg shape. By placing strips of tape at each end of the halves, the children will secure both flaps. Ask students to write two or three clues about the identity of their chosen animal on the lines beneath the egg. Display all the drawings and riddles on a bulletin board titled "Guess Who's Hatching?" Children will enjoy trying to figure out the answer to their classmates' riddles, then lifting the flaps to peek inside the eggs to see if they were correct.

Eggshell Art: Ask students to bring in clean, rinsed eggshells to use in making spring-themed mosaics. Break the eggshells into small pieces and divide them among six cups. Use commercial dyes to tint the shells, and allow them to dry thoroughly. Ask students to create outline drawings of simple spring scenes. They can then "paint" the scene by gluing different colored eggshells in place on their drawings.

Who?

Who lives inside a house
that doesn't have a door?

It doesn't have a window
or light inside, what's more.

Who lives inside a house
with walls so frail and thin
that when he once comes out
he cannot go back in?

—Aileen Fisher

May

Maytime Magic

Poetry Pointers

After reading the poem, ask students what phrase they hear repeated. Point out that the repetition of the phrase "a little" creates rhythm and music in the poem. Children may enjoy inventing a finger play to accompany another reading of the poem. Experiment with hand gestures that might be used with each line.

Inspirations

Ready, Set, Grow: Students can observe "Maytime Magic" firsthand by planting windowsill gardens and watching them grow. Divide children into groups, and provide each group with an egg carton, eggshell halves (rinsed and dried) to line each compartment, soil, and seeds. Different groups might want to choose different kinds of seeds to grow, for example, fruit, vegetables, herbs, flowers, or legumes. Children can label each compartment of the egg carton by writing the type of seed on a strip of paper, taping it to a toothpick, and pushing it into the soil. Groups can record seed developments in their science journals and compare results they have with the different seeds. The eggshell containers can later be planted directly in the soil outdoors and will provide nourishment for growing seedlings. Encourage children to continue monitoring the progress of their gardens.

In the Garden: Here's a fun and challenging spring-themed listening activity: Divide students into groups, and have groups sit in circles in different parts of the room. Children can clap their hands on their thighs to keep the rhythm going for the following chant:

"In the garden, in the garden, what shall we grow in the garden?"

After chanting the chorus, students should pause as one child names an item to grow, for example, "I'm going to grow carrots." The group then repeats the chorus, pausing to let the next child repeat the name of the first item in the garden and add a new item, for example, "I'm going to grow carrots and daisies." Children should continue around the circle naming things they will grow in the garden, however they must first name all of the items previously mentioned. As the game proceeds, it becomes more challenging. When one child forgets to name an item, or mixes up the order of items, that round of the game ends and a new round begins.

Maytime Magic

A little seed
For me to sow . . .

A little earth
To make it grow . . .
A little hole,
A little pat . . .
A little wish,
And that is that.

A little sun,
A little shower . . .
A little while,
And then—a flower!

—Mabel Watts

Ladybug · Fireflies · Spider

Poetry Pointers

Omit the title for each of these short poems when you read them aloud and
have children try to guess the type of bug each is about. What clues in each
poem did they base their guesses on? These are all examples of *haiku*. If children aren't familiar with haiku poetry, you may want to provide them with some
background information about the form. Japanese in origin, haiku are typically
mini-snapshots of the natural world, although modern poets write haiku on
every topic. Haiku often link an element in nature with some aspect of human
nature. The poems often follow a pattern of syllables, with 5 syllables in the first
line, 7 in the second, and 5 in the third. However, traditionally it is acceptable
to have a short line, followed by a longer line, followed by another short line.
Explain to students that a syllable is one beat of sound. Then reread each haiku
slowly and invite children to clap out the syllables.

Inspirations

Insect Anatomy: Not all of the bugs in the poems are insects. Discuss the basics
of insect anatomy with children: All insects have three body parts (a head, a
thorax, and an abdomen), six legs, and antennae (feelers) on their head. Invite
children to do some detective work. Can they figure out which bug among those
featured in the haiku is not an insect? *(the spider)* How can they tell? Have
children do further research about specific bugs, those in the haiku as well as
others in which they are interested. Distribute unlined index cards to students.
On one side, they can draw a picture of their chosen bug. On the other, they can
write a few interesting facts about it. Punch holes in the index cards and suspend
them from a hanger using yarn in varying lengths to create a "Bug Mobile."

Bug Watchers: If possible, take children to a park or garden and let them
watch bugs up close. Encourage students to make notes and drawings in their
science journals. Back in the classroom, students can use these notes to help
them write their own bug haiku. Before children begin writing, invite them to
think of the way a camera captures a split second in time. Remind them that
haiku do the same thing, telling about just one moment in nature. Children
may enjoy creating watercolor paintings to illustrate their haiku. Allow the
paintings to dry overnight. Then help children copy their poems in black felt-
tipped pen onto their pictures for an effect reminiscent of traditional Japanese
watercolor painting.

Ladybug

Look! A red raindrop
Shimmering on a daisy
Has sprouted wings!

Fireflies

Tiny, twinkling stars
Play a game of hide-and-seek
by the backyard fence

Spider

Between two green stems
You spread your lace tablecloth
And prepare to dine

—Maria Fleming

Whale

Poetry Pointers

Invite students to find all the words in the poem that mean the same thing as *fat* (*stout, enormous, chubby*). You may want to tell children that these words are called *synonyms*. Can they think of any other synonyms for the word *fat* to add to the list? Next, ask children to identify all the words in the poem that name a family relationship (*daughters, sons, uncles, aunts, nephews, nieces*). Point out that the poet lists all these relationships to add humor to the poem.

Inspirations

Hooray for Blubber!: There's a good reason for a whale to be pleased with its layers of fat: They keep it warm in the icy ocean. Tell children that this fat is called *blubber*. Students can try this science experiment to see just how fat fights the cold:

1. Put 2½ cups of solid vegetable shortening in the bottom of a self-sealing plastic sandwich bag.

2. Turn a second self-sealing plastic sandwich bag inside out, then place it inside the first bag.

3. Zip the two bags together, making sure they lock.

4. Spread the shortening around until it completely surrounds the interior bag.

5. Place the "blubber bag" on one hand. Place both hands in a tub of ice water.

Ask: Which hand feels warmer? Why? How would this help whales survive in the icy ocean waters?

Sizing Up Whales: Just how big are whales? While whales are all large creatures, they vary widely in length. Beluga whales, for example, are about 16 feet long, while the biggest whale, the blue whale, can grow to be 100 feet long. To help children envision just how enormous the blue whale is, have them measure out the distance in a long hallway or on a playground. Mark the beginning and ending point of your measurement with a chalk line. Divide children into pairs, and have partners measure each other's height using a piece of string. Students can then determine how many children their height could lie end to end on the back of a blue whale by seeing how many times they can stretch the string between the two line markers.

Whale

A whale is stout about the middle,
He is stout about the ends,
& so is all his family
& so are all his friends.

He's pleased that he's enormous,
He's happy he weighs tons,
& so are all his daughters
& so are all his sons.

He eats when he is hungry
Each kind of food he wants,
& so do all his uncles
& so do all his aunts.

He doesn't mind his blubber,
He doesn't mind his creases,
& neither do his nephews
& neither do his nieces.

You may find him chubby,
You may find him fat,
But he would disagree with you:
He likes himself like that.

—Mary Ann Hoberman

Tree House Night

Poetry Pointers

The poet uses simile and metaphor to capture the experience of sleeping in a tree house on a moonlit night. Ask children to listen for the comparisons that the poet makes. (In line 6, the moon is compared to an owl's eye. In line 9, she calls the stars "silver fireworks." In line 15, the narrator of the poem curls up "like a squirrel in a nest.")

Inspirations

Giving Trees: Secret hiding places and homes for animals are just two of the ways trees are used by people and animals. Enlist children's help to create a display that shows some of the other reasons we need trees. To prepare for the activity, photocopy the leaf patterns on the reproducible on page 121 onto green construction paper. On long sheets of craft paper, draw the outline of a tree's trunk and a few branches and paint them brown. On the leaf patterns, children can write the many gifts that trees give the world, including food, lumber, air to breathe, homes for animals, beauty, and so on. Cut out the leaf shapes and paste them to the tree's branches to finish the display.

Just Me, Myself, and I: Do children have a special spot they like to go to be alone, think, read, dream, rest, or even cry? Ask children to write a sentence or two about their favorite place at the bottom of a sheet of paper. Invite them to use a comparison to describe their favorite place, as the poet does in "Tree House Night." For example, "My favorite place is our big blue stuffed chair. I feel cozy like a bird in its nest." Children can then draw pictures of themselves in their favorite spot. Compile their pages into a class book called "Our Favorite Places."

Tree House Night

At night I climbed
the ladder
to my house
up in the tree.
The moon was like
an owl's eye
staring down at me.
The stars
were silver fireworks
that never burned away.
The robins' bedtime
songs were done . . .
they rested for the day.
I rolled up in my blanket
like a squirrel in a nest.
I knew my dreams
this cool-moon night
would be the very best.

—Sandra Liatsos

June

Butterfly Wings

Poetry Pointers

After reading the poem, ask children what change has taken place between the first and last stanzas. (A caterpillar has changed into a butterfly.) Ask children if they have ever seen a butterfly in flight. How is a butterfly's flight different from that of birds? What does the poet compare a butterfly in flight to? *(a boat at sea)* Can children think of anything else to compare a butterfly's flight to? List their comparisons on chart paper.

Inspirations

Life-Cycle Wheels: Set up a reading corner that features a variety of books about butterflies, including nonfiction titles that describe the process of *metamorphosis*. Children can then make life-cycle wheels to illustrate this transformation. Begin by providing students with two paper plates. Show students how to draw lines dividing the surface of both plates into four equal parts. Students should then draw, in sequence, each of the four stages (egg, caterpillar, chrysalis, butterfly) in a butterfly's life cycle on one of the plates. Next, cut away one of the four quadrants on the other plate. Place this plate on top of the first plate. The sides with the quadrant lines should face each other. Help children poke a small hole through the center of the stacked plates, then attach them with a brass fastener. By turning the bottom plate, children can reveal the pictures one by one. Invite students to use the life-cycle wheels as visual aids to explain in their own words the stages of a butterfly's life.

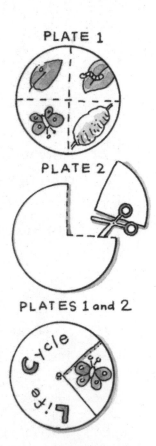

Beautiful Butterflies: Children can make beautiful, fluttery butterflies using coffee filters and clothespins. First, dilute a couple drops of food coloring in a tablespoon of water. Repeat this with several colors. Using eyedroppers, students can splash droplets of the "paint" onto coffee filters. Encourage children to experiment with different colors to create patterns. Allow the coffee filters to dry, then gather them in the middle and clasp with a clothespin to create wings. Attach the butterflies to a clothesline to brighten your classroom.

Butterfly Wings

How would it be
on a day in June
to open your eyes
in a dark cocoon,

And soften one end
and crawl outside,
and find you had wings
to open wide,

And find you could fly
to a bush or tree
or float on the air
like a boat at sea . . .

How would it BE?

—Aileen Fisher

Sunflower, Sunflower

Poetry Pointers

Ask children if they notice anything unusual about this poem. (The rhymes come at the beginning or middle of a line, not at the end.) Using different colored markers, students can underline the words that rhyme in each stanza. Which stanzas contain three rhyming words? (stanzas 1, 3, and 5) Which contain only two? (stanzas 2 and 4)

Inspirations

A Garden of Rhymes: Refer children back to the rhyming words they underlined in the poem. Divide the class into small groups, and provide each group with a copy of the flower pattern on the reproducible on page 122. Write the following words from the poem (or other words you choose) on slips of paper and put them in a hat: *sun, proud, light, high, eat, seed.* Have groups select one of the words and write it in the center of their flower patterns. Groups should then brainstorm rhyming words, writing each one on a petal. Invite groups to fill all of the petals. They can color their flowers, cut them out, and tape them to wooden dowels. Show children how to wrap the dowels with green crepe paper and attach paper leaves. "Plant" the dowels in a windowsill garden trough or pails filled with dirt or sand. Use this activity as an opportunity to look at the different spelling patterns for each family of rhyming words.

Good Enough to Eat: Draw students' attention to the last line of the poem. Have they ever eaten sunflower seeds? Tell children that seeds are just one part of plants that we eat. Review the parts of a plant, including seed, root, stem, leaf, flower, and fruit. Together, generate a list of plant foods we eat. Then create a class chart that groups these foods according to plant part, for example:

SEED	ROOT	STEM	LEAF	FLOWER	FRUIT
sunflower seeds	potatoes	asparagus	spinach	broccoli	tomatoes
peanuts	carrots	celery	lettuce	cauliflower	oranges
peas	radishes			apples	
beans	turnips			berries	

Sunflower, Sunflower

Sunflower
fun flower
you're
      my favorite one flower.

Full flower
proud flower
you're
      my shout-out-loud-flower.

Light flower
bright flower
you're
      my sun-at-night-flower.

Wide flower
high flower
you're
      my scrape-the-sky-flower.

Sunflower
fun flower
you're my
      eat-the-seeds-when-done-flower.

        —Robert Heidbreder

Cow

Poetry Pointers

"Cow" is what's known as a *persona* poem. In persona poems, the poet speaks in the voice of his or her subject, in this case, a cow. Cover up the title of the poem and read it aloud to children. Ask them to identify who is speaking. The poem also makes good use of the technique of *assonance*, which is the repetition of an internal vowel sound. Reread the poem, emphasizing the long *ooooh* sound whenever you come upon it, for example in the words *approve, June, chew, move,* and *too*. Ask students what this long "ooooh" sound reminds them of. (the "moo" sound a cow makes) Tell them that the poet was being playful and wanted the speaker to sound like a cow talking. Children will enjoy exaggerating the *ooooh* sounds with you during another reading of the poem. Together, make a list of all the words that contain the *ooooh* sound and examine the different spelling patterns that create it.

Inspirations

Milk and More: Read children *The Milk Makers* by Gail Gibbons (Atheneum, 1985) to help them understand how milk gets from the cow to their refrigerator. Find a picture of a cow and staple it to the center of a bulletin board. Draw lines emanating from the cow in all directions. Provide children with magazines and ask them to hunt for pictures of different milk products, then cut them out. Invite students to find as many different milk products as possible, such as whole milk, skim milk, chocolate milk, cream, cheese, ice cream, butter, evaporated milk, powdered milk, yogurt, cottage cheese, cream cheese, buttermilk, sour cream, and so on.

Persona Poems: Children will get a kick out of assuming the identity and voice of other animals as they write their own persona poems. Before students begin writing, allow time for them to research the behavior of an animal that interests them and closely study its appearance. Encourage children to also imagine, and make notes about, the animal's "personality," as well as its fears, hopes, pleasures, and dreams. Children can incorporate some of these ideas into their poems. Suggest that students imitate Marilyn Singer's technique of including words that echo the sound their animal makes. For example, a poem about a snake might feature lots of words that include the letter "s," to echo a snake's hissing sound; a poem in the voice of a sheep might exaggerate the "ah" sound in some words to imitate its trademark *baaaaah*. Invite students to share their poems with classmates. They may want to leave out their poem's title to see if their classmates can guess what animal they wrote about.

Cow

I approve of June
Fresh food to chew
   and chew
   and chew
Lots of room to move around
   or lie down
Not too hot
Not too cold
Not too wet
Not too dry
A good roof of sky over me and my calf
Who's now halfway up
   on new legs
He'll want a meal real soon
Yes, I approve of June

–Marilyn Singer

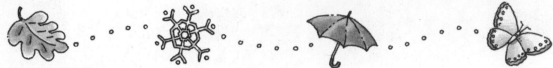

Popsicle

Poetry Pointers

"Popsicle" is a *concrete poem*—it takes the shape of its subject matter. It also uses playful language, some of which is invented to create whimsical, musical rhymes. On a second reading, ask students to listen for some of these made-up words. Also, point out the clever positioning of the word *sticky*. Ask children what word is formed by dropping the letter "y" from *sticky*. *(stick)* What part of the popsicle does the word form? *(the popsicle stick)*

Inspirations

Summer Fun: Licking an icy, drippy popsicle on a hot day is one of summer's many pleasures. What else do students like about summer? What are they looking forward to seeing, eating, and doing during this summer break? Provide children with unlined index cards. Ask children to imagine themselves in July. Where will they be and what will they be doing? They can then use the index cards to create postcards, addressed to you, family members, or classmates, with a picture on the front and a message on the back. The postcards need not depict a vacation locale; they can simply show children playing in their neighborhoods or at the local park. Display the cards along a clothesline in your classroom.

Shaping Up: Students may enjoy writing their own concrete poems. Encourage them to pick something that has as simple a shape as the subject of their poem. A raindrop, star, heart, leaf, sun, cloud, and butterfly are some ideas to try. Children should write the first draft of their poem without regard to shape. Next, they can draw lightly in pencil the outlined shape of their poem's subject matter and write the poem inside. It may take a few more drafts before children get the lines to break and fill the shape the way they want them to. When students have arranged things to their liking, they can erase the pencil outline and let the words themselves suggest the shape.

Popsicle

popsicle
popsicle
tickle
tongue fun
licksicle
sticksicle
please
don't run
dripsicle
slipsicle
melt, melt
tricky
stopsicle
plopsicle
hand all
sticky

—Joan Bransfield Graham

Butterfly Buddies

Sizing Up Pumpkins

Ready! Set! Read!

Follow the directions below to make a bookmark. Color a dinosaur for every book you read during National Book Week.

ℰ Cut out the bookmark and fold.
ℰ Turn the bookmark over and coat the other side lightly with glue.
ℰ Fold the two pasted halves together.
ℰ Tuck it in your favorite book!

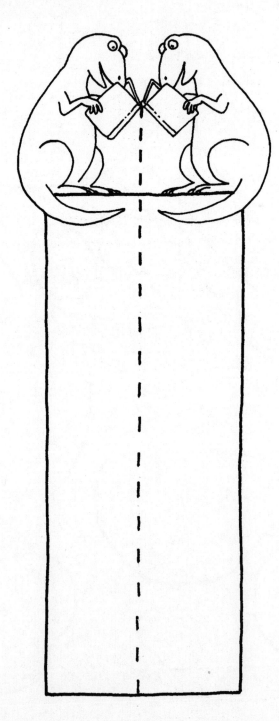

The Bear Facts

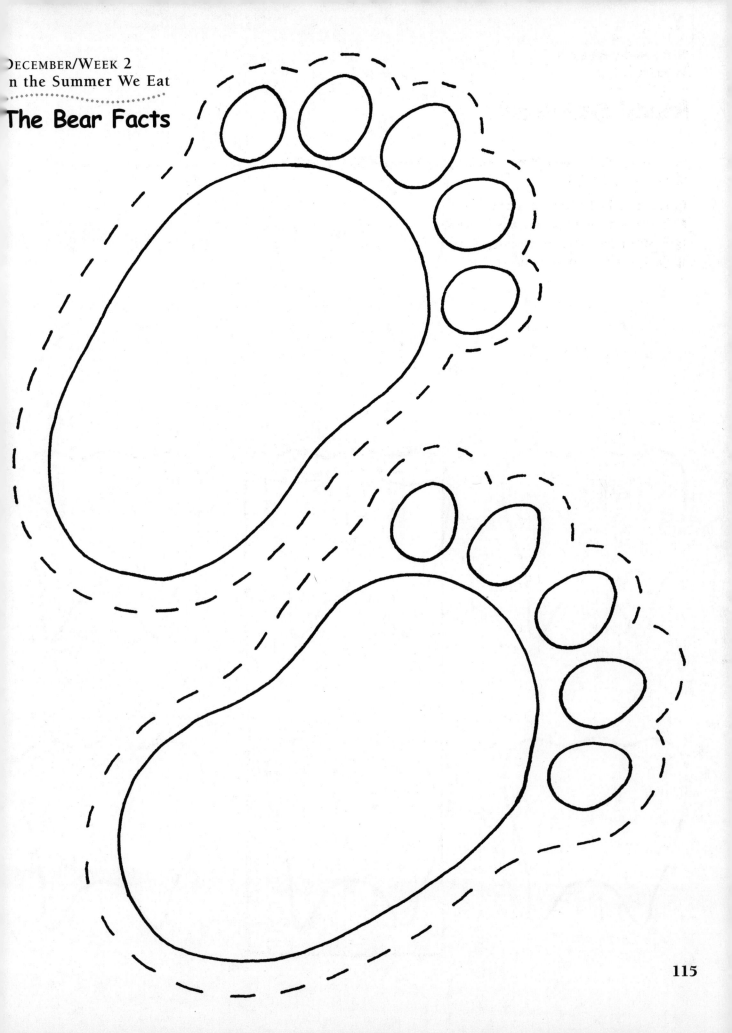

Tooth Count

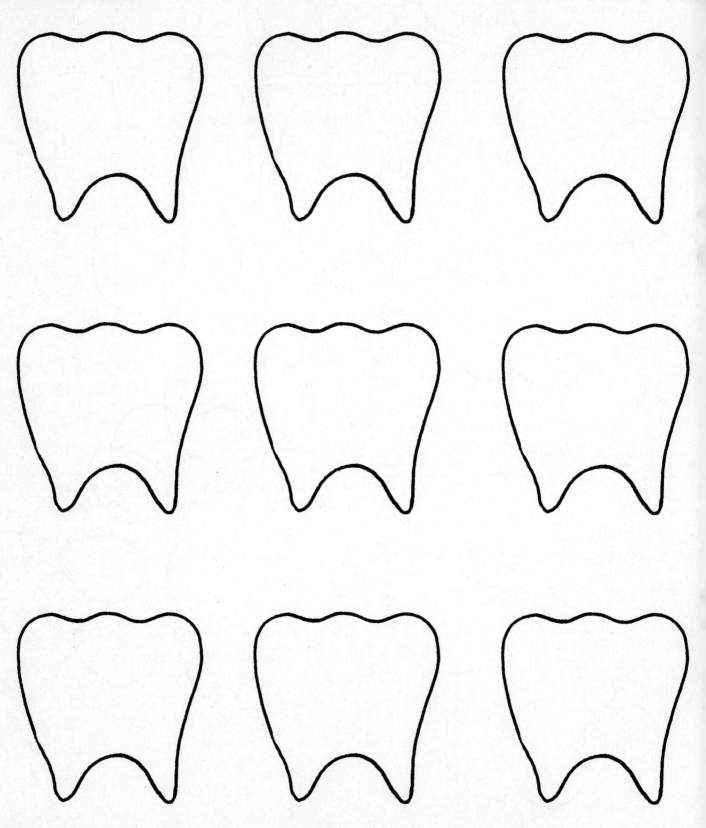

Luck of the Irish

Wet-Weather Words

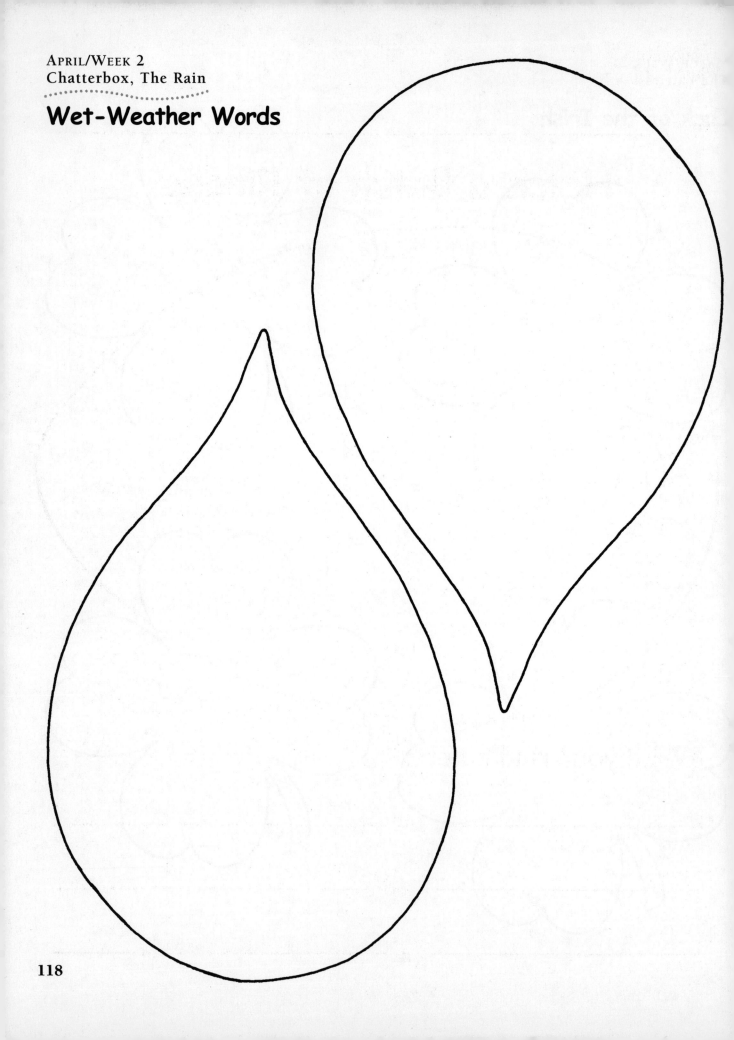

Name _____

Hatch a Batch of Riddles

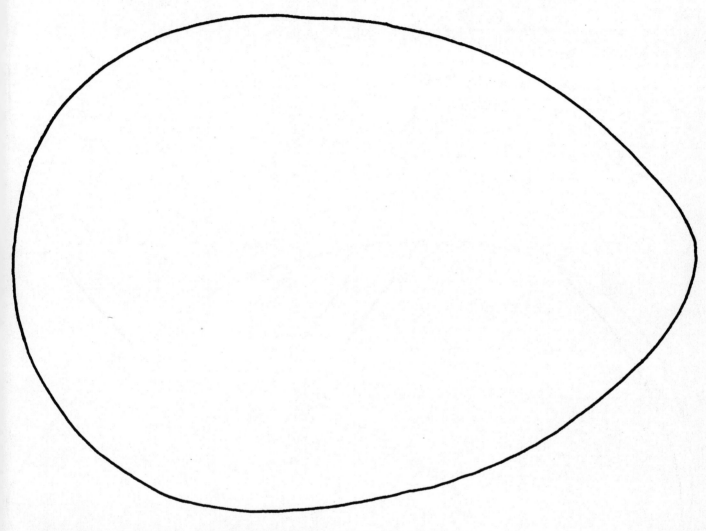

Write your riddle here:

_____

_____

_____

Hatch a Batch of Riddles

Follow the directions below.

@ Cut out the cracked egg shape.
@ Cover your drawing on page 119 with the cracked egg.
@ Tape along the dotted lines found on both ends of the cracked egg.
@ Fold back each half of the cracked egg to reveal your riddle's answer.

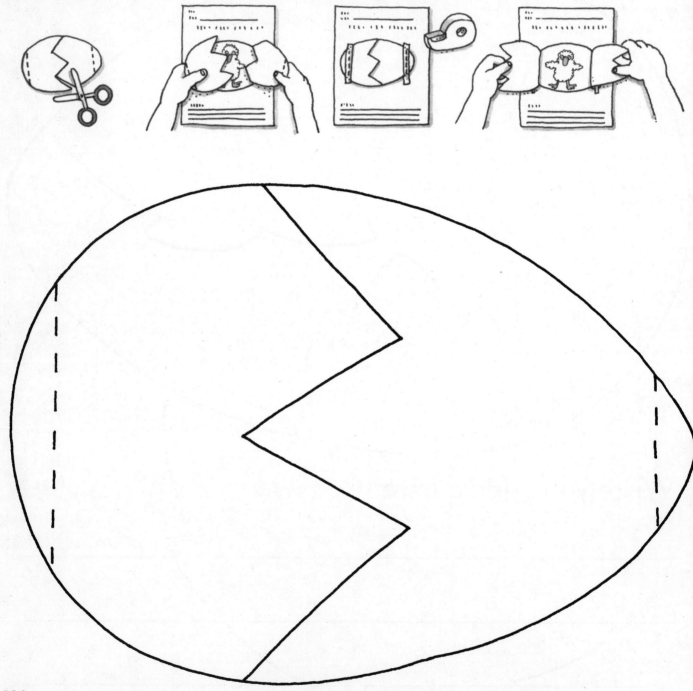

Giving Trees

A Garden of Rhymes

Notes

Notes

Notes

Notes

Notes

Notes